INEZ & VINOODH

I See You in Everything

HATJE CANTZ

The Ravestijn Gallery is proud to present *I See You in Everything,* the first solo exhibition at the gallery of the artist duo, Inez van Lamsweerde and Vinoodh Matadin, better known by their collaborative name Inez & Vinoodh. Without a singular theme or period, the exhibition will comprise of an array of work selected from a colossal career that sprawls over thirty years including photographs made for *Vogue* Paris, *New York Times Magazine, Purple* and *The Face.*

Such a myriad of work is emblematic of Inez & Vinoodh; unrestricted by a fixed aesthetic and allowing their approach to be determined by those in front of the camera, the idea behind each photograph always takes precedence. Each work is authored by their collective name and by eschewing further information of their individual roles, we are reminded of their de-votion to the image and the person, rather than to context and expectation. And whilst their methodology is constantly responding and fluctuating, it is a persistent duality (both in their artistic work and in life as partners) that creates their unifying and unmistakable character. As Inez says herself, "there's always a tension between the beautiful and the grotesque, the spiritual and the mundane, high fashion and low fashion, male and female." Indeed, this duality can be seen in many of the photographs included in the exhibition. In *Lucy Fer,* the Estonian supermodel Carmen Kass is transmuted into a mythological three-headed creature; a vast flood of wiry-haired faces sits atop her naked body and here the elegance and realism of the human form is pitted against monstrous fantasy.

Dualism remains the nuanced personality of Inez & Vinoodh's work but what is fundamental to their emergence is the pair's pioneering use of digital technologies. In the early 1990s, they were the first to use software to mould their own, idiosyncratic vision in the context of fashion, beginning with the series *For Your Pleasure,* published in the April 1994 Issue of *The Face.* Flamboyant, stylised models were digitally pasted onto a swathe of stock images to create bizarre and audacious photographs that demonstrated a thoughtful embrace of a now often-viewed problematic paradigm shift. A Two-Tone Stretch Satin and Lace Pantsuit by Bertrand Marechal, another work on show in the exhibition, portrays a woman, dressed in a lustrous low-cut pantsuit and in a state of ecstasy, stood next to and holding the t-shirt of an ingenuous, smiling boy sat on a doctor's bed. The manipulation of the two images is balanced in such an astute manner that we are able to notice the hand of Inez & Vinoodh only just, allowing us to suspend our disbelief, if only for a moment. Although this way of working no longer dominates their oeuvre, often traded for a sensibility built entirely in the real, such a context is critical to understanding their art as a relentless dedication to the photographic medium.

Their maverick ways of working have facilitated a new perception of fashion photographs in the context of art, seeing their work grace the pages of fashion magazines and the walls of museums in equal measure. Thirty years on, Inez & Vinoodh still taunt the temporality of much modern fashion, trading trends for timeless photographs, some which are re-contextualised decades later, just as this exhibition intends to do.

THE RAVESTIJN GALLERY

Lady Gaga / Mel, 2015

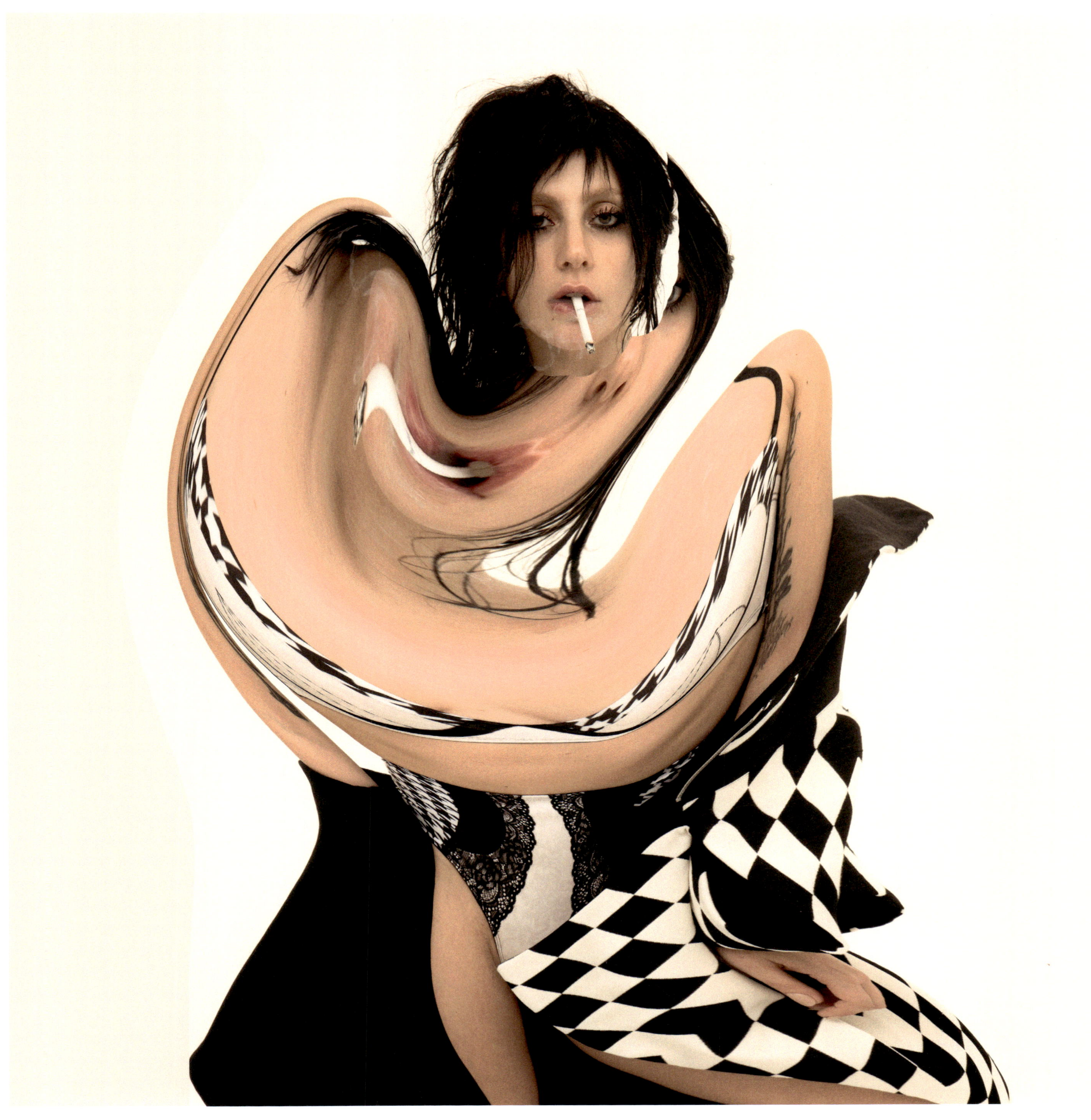

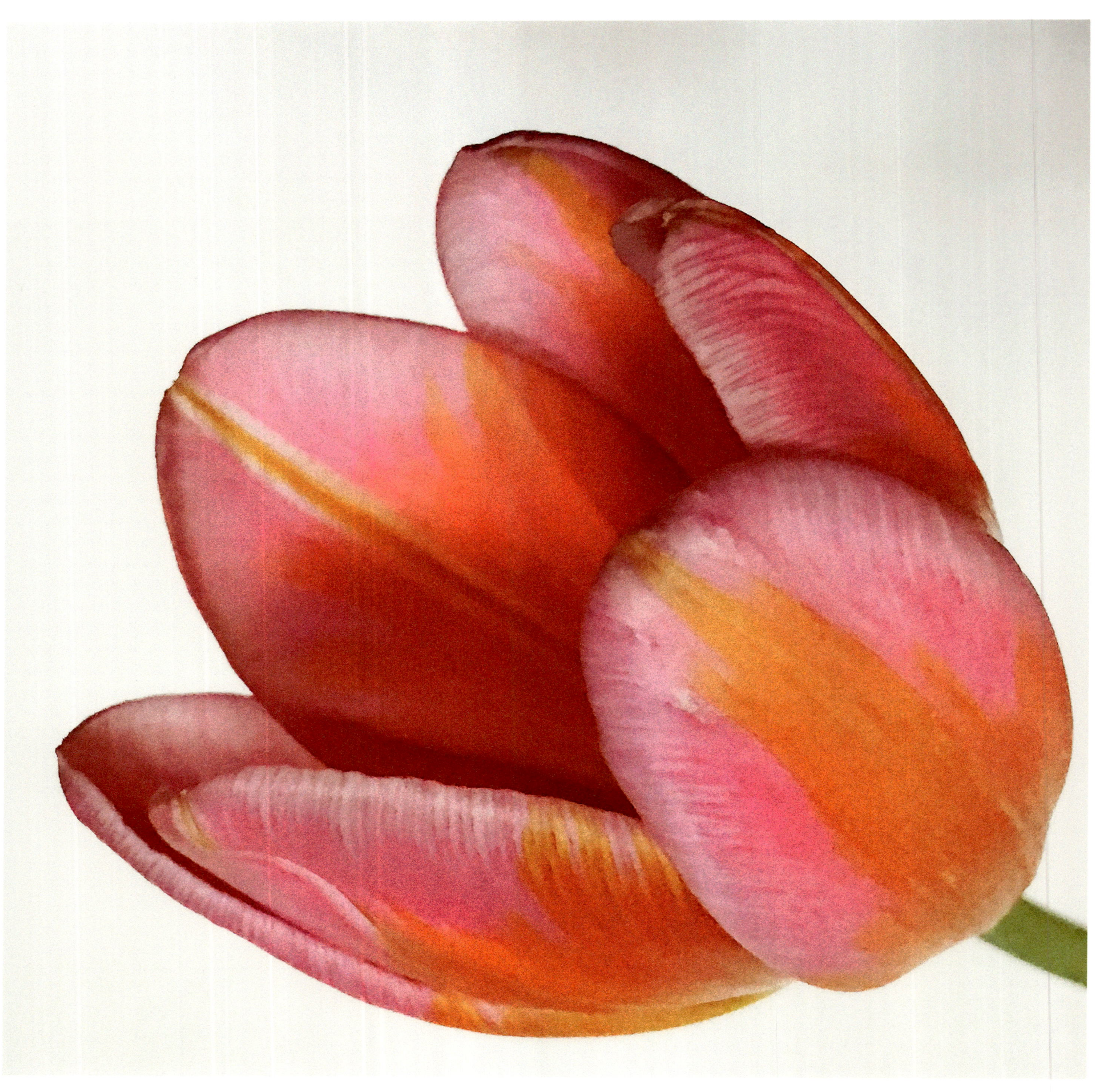

Hiandra Martinez, 2017

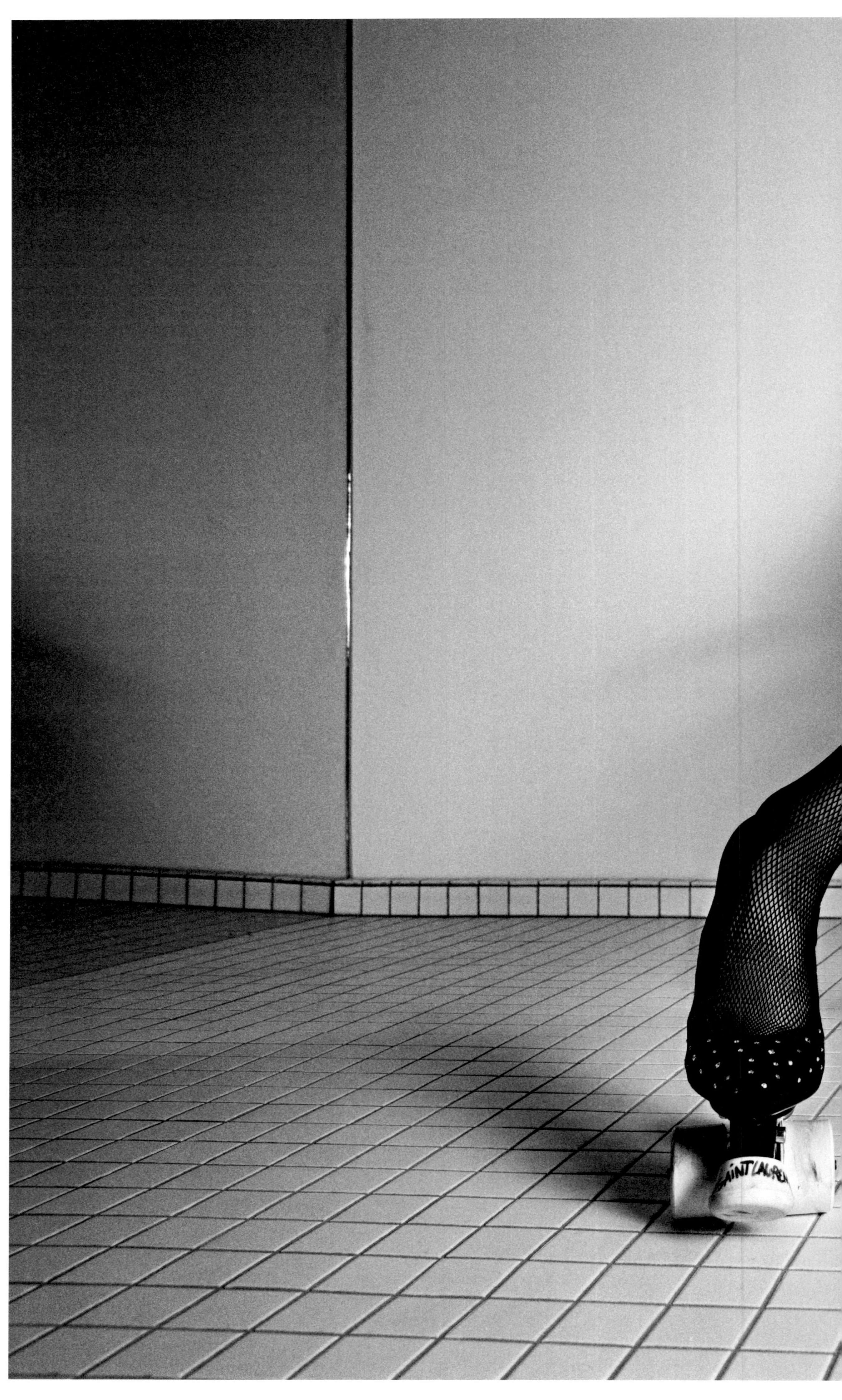

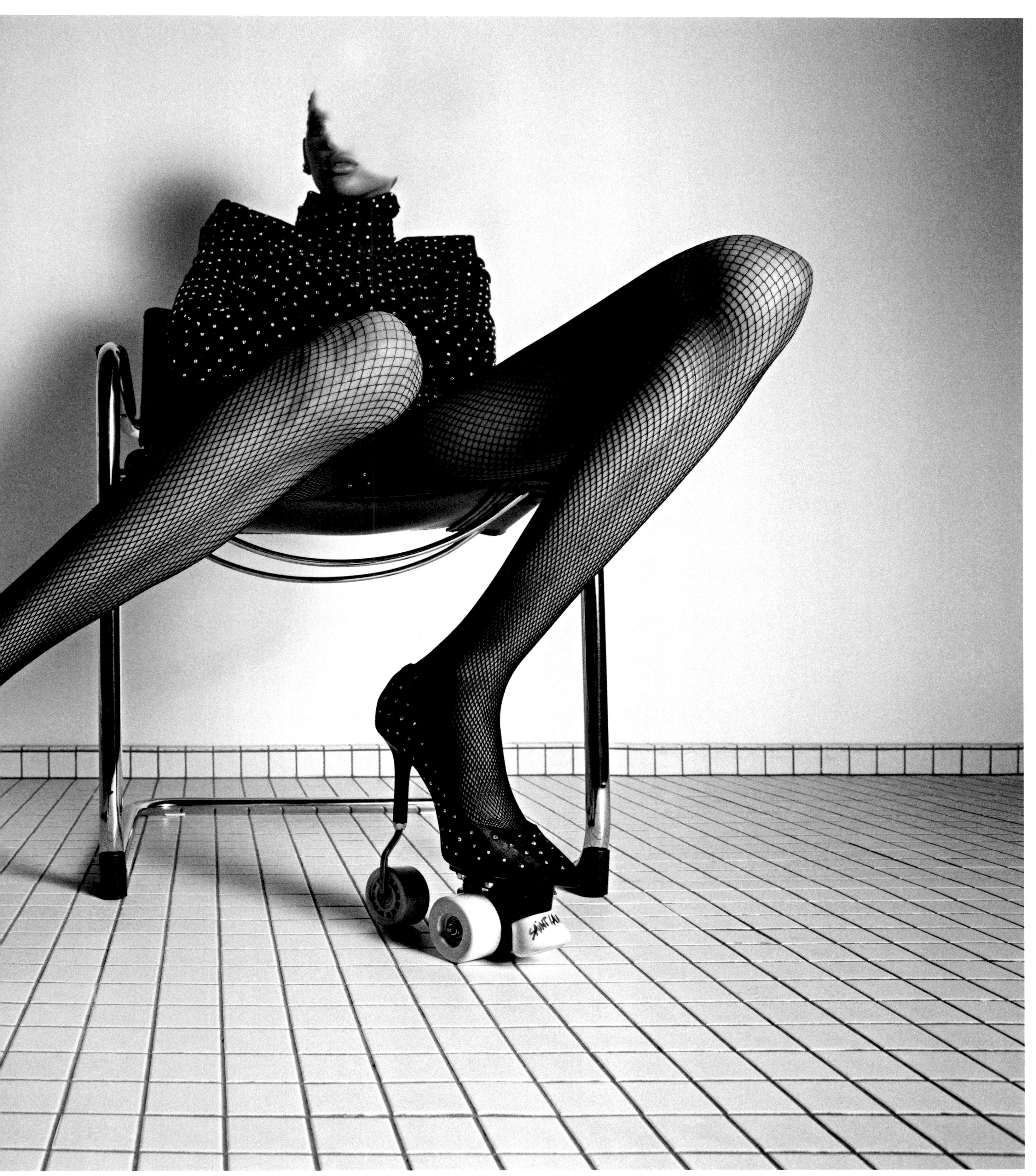

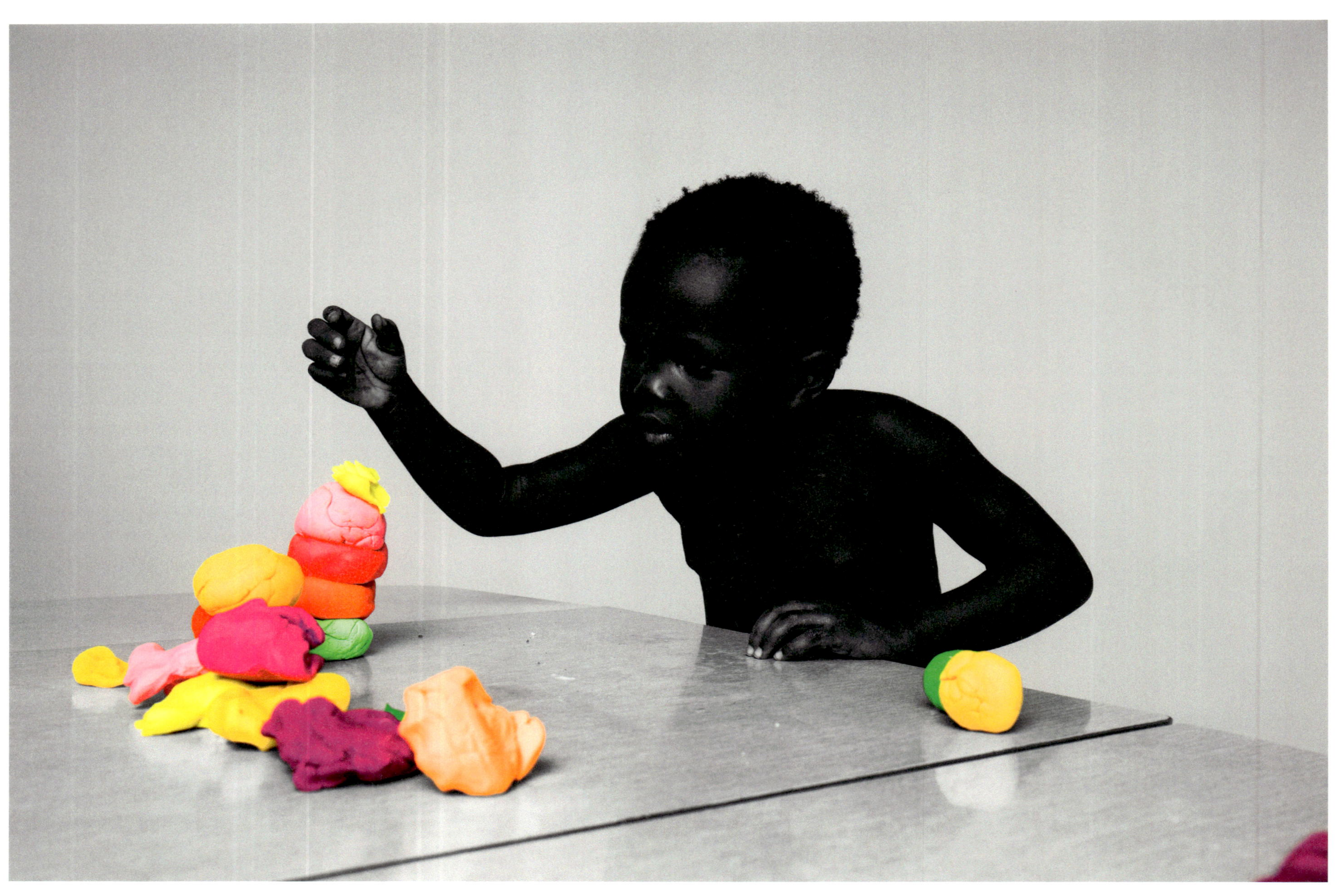

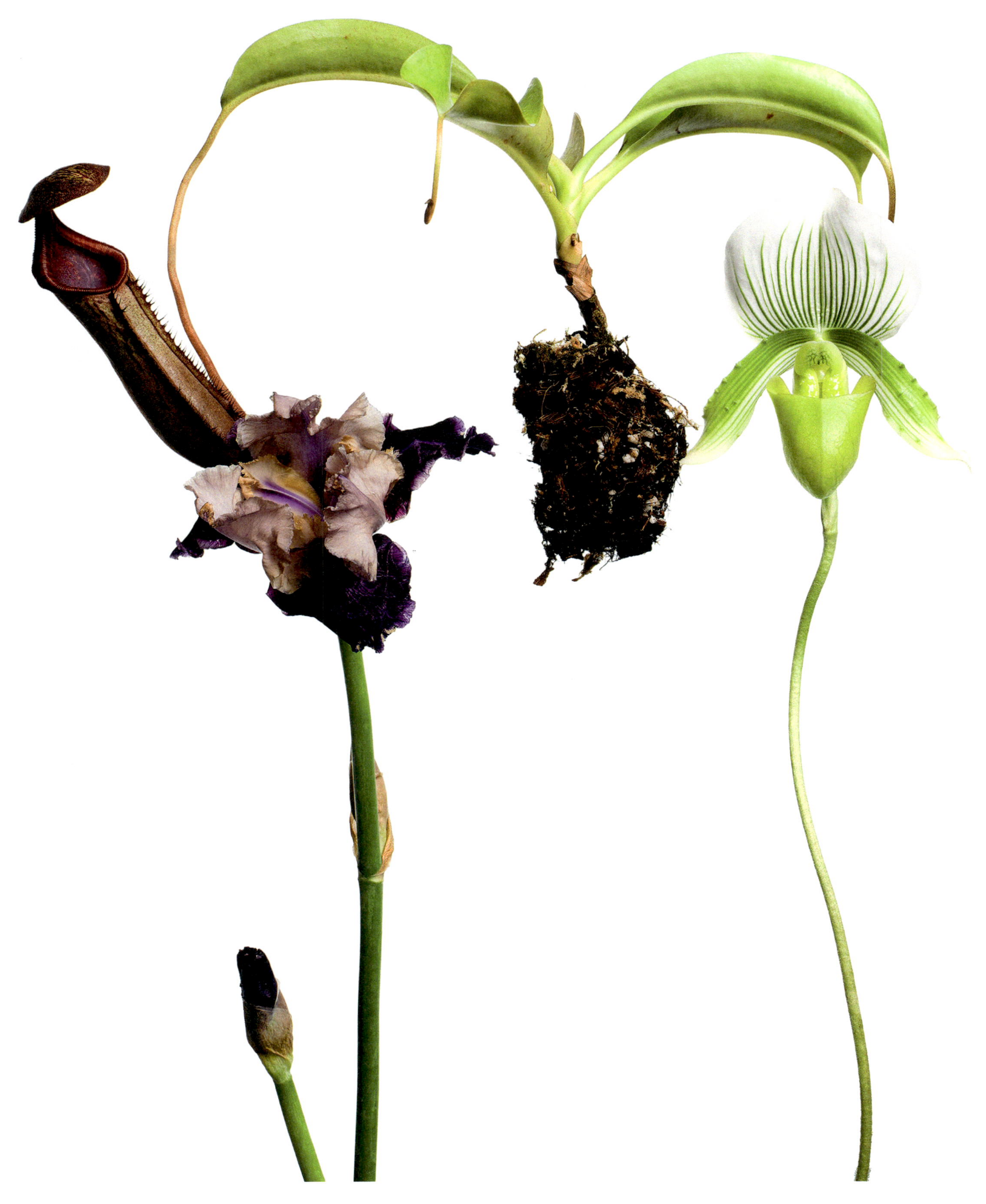

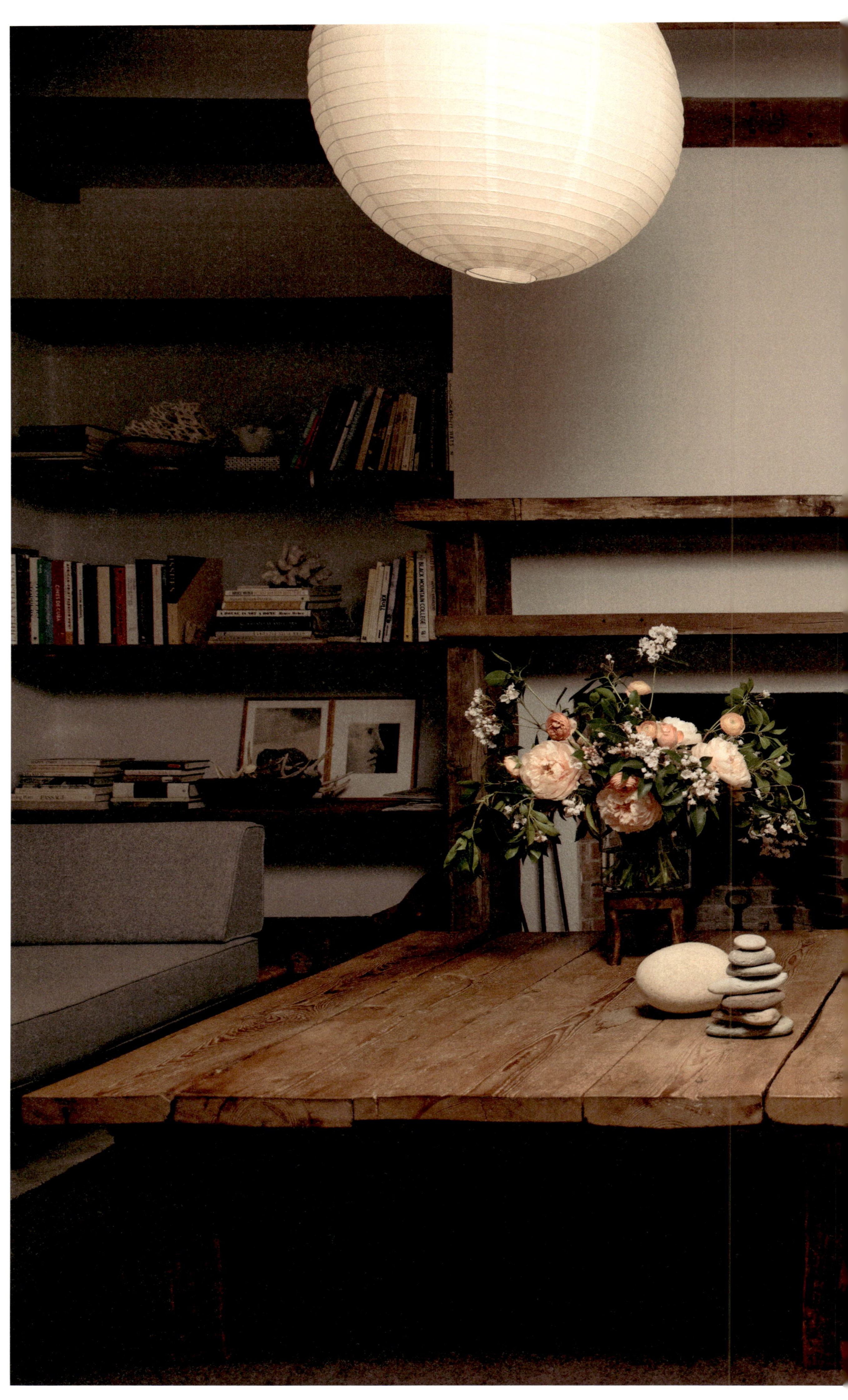

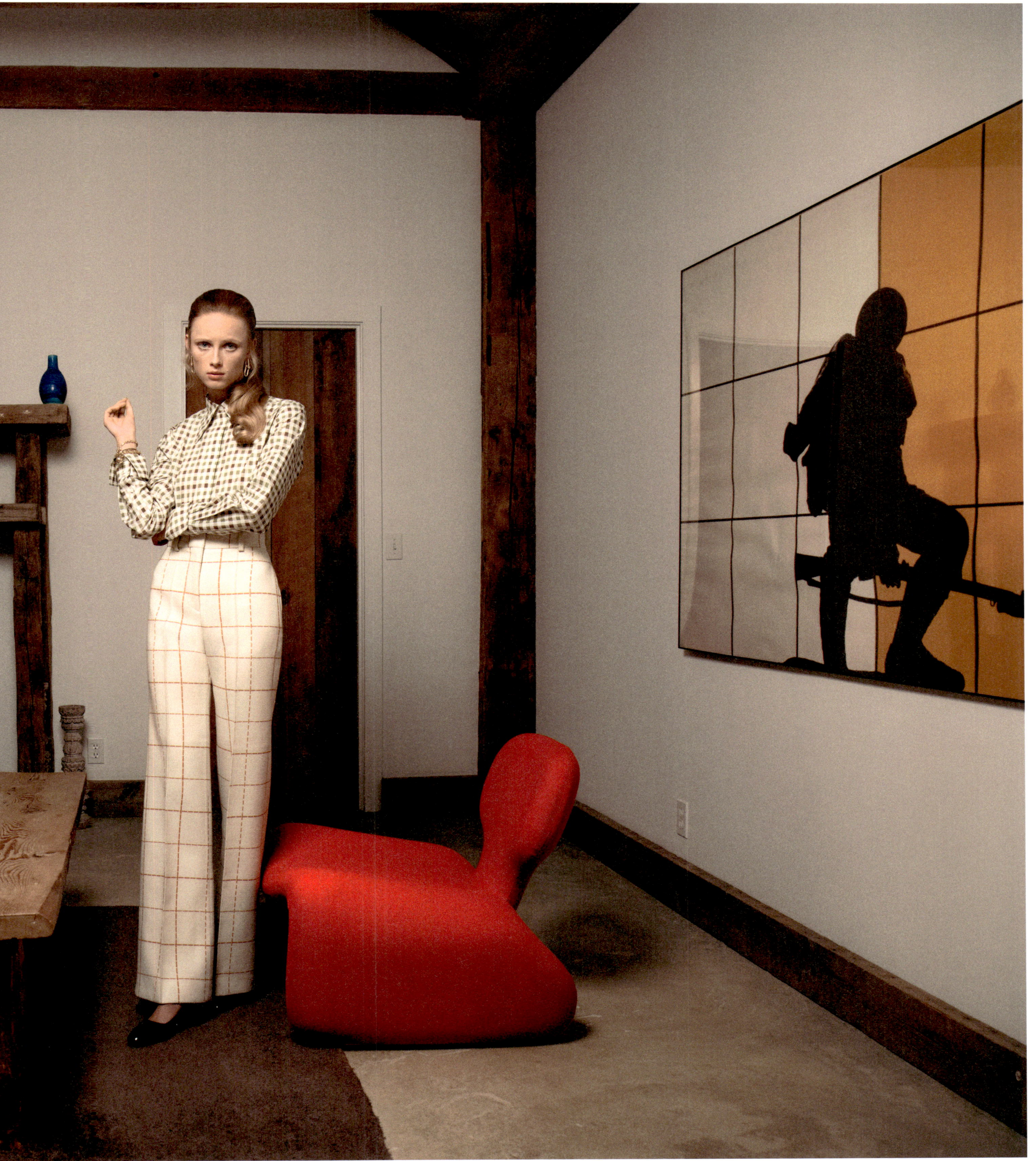

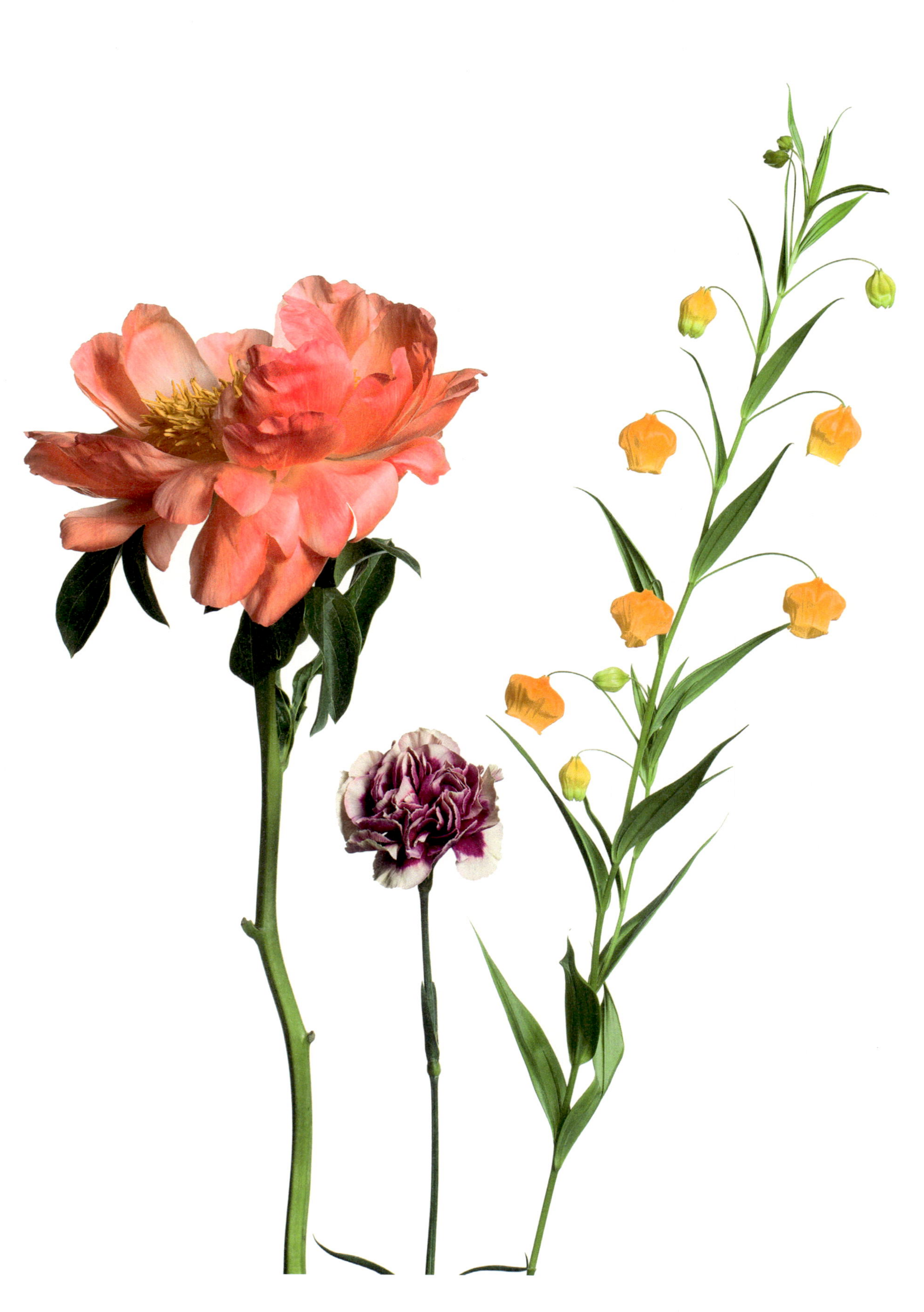

1 Pink Peony, 1 Two Tone Carnation, 1 Sandersonia, 2013

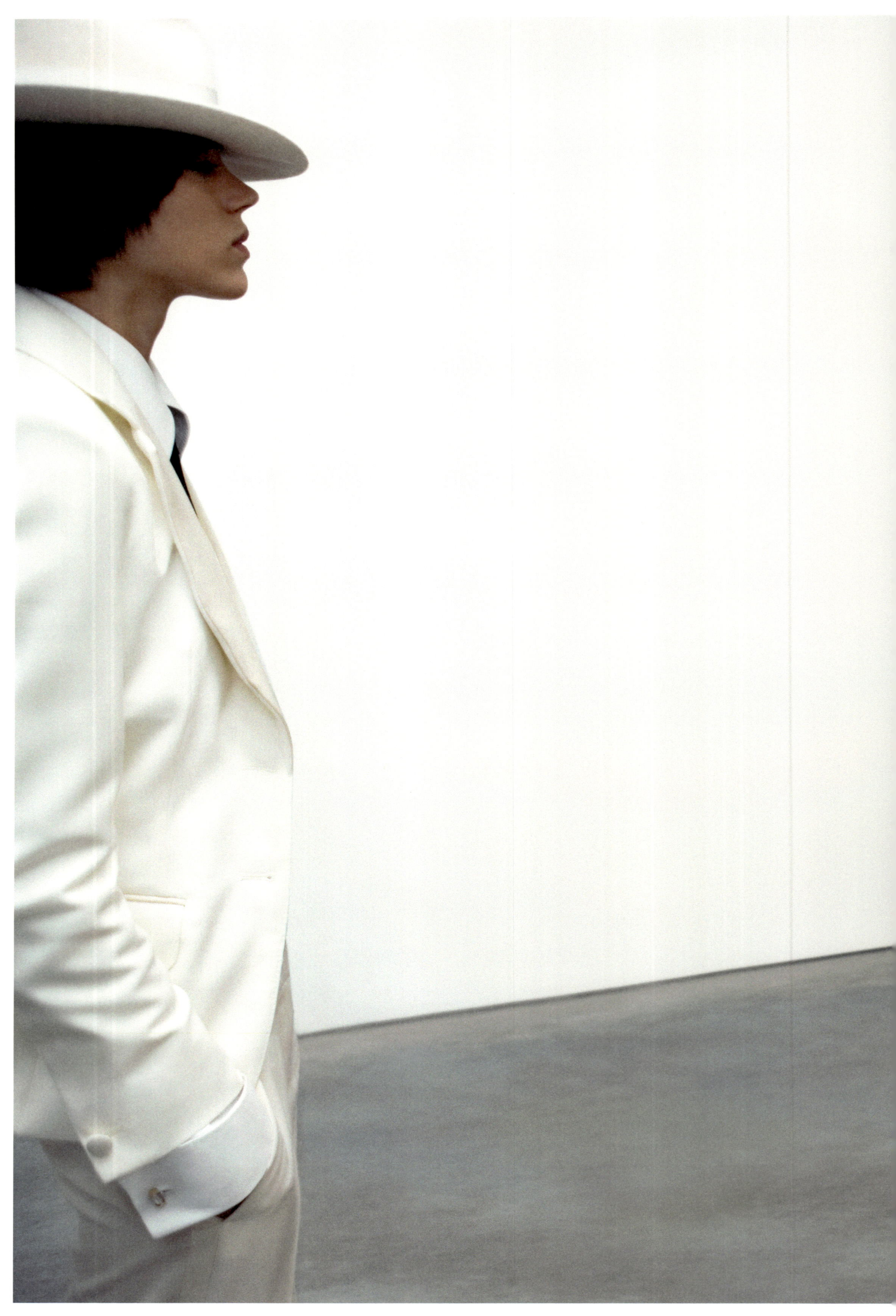

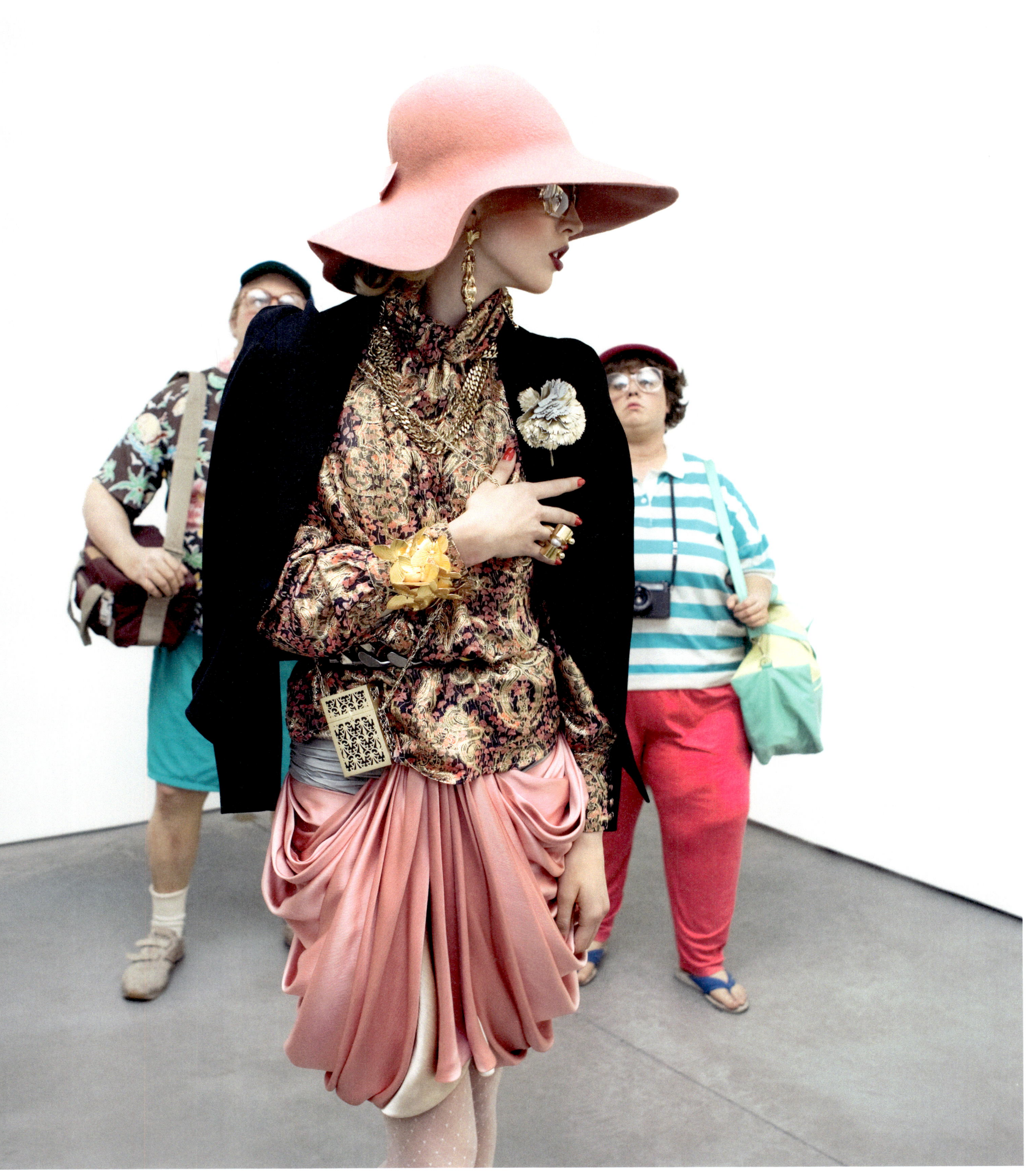

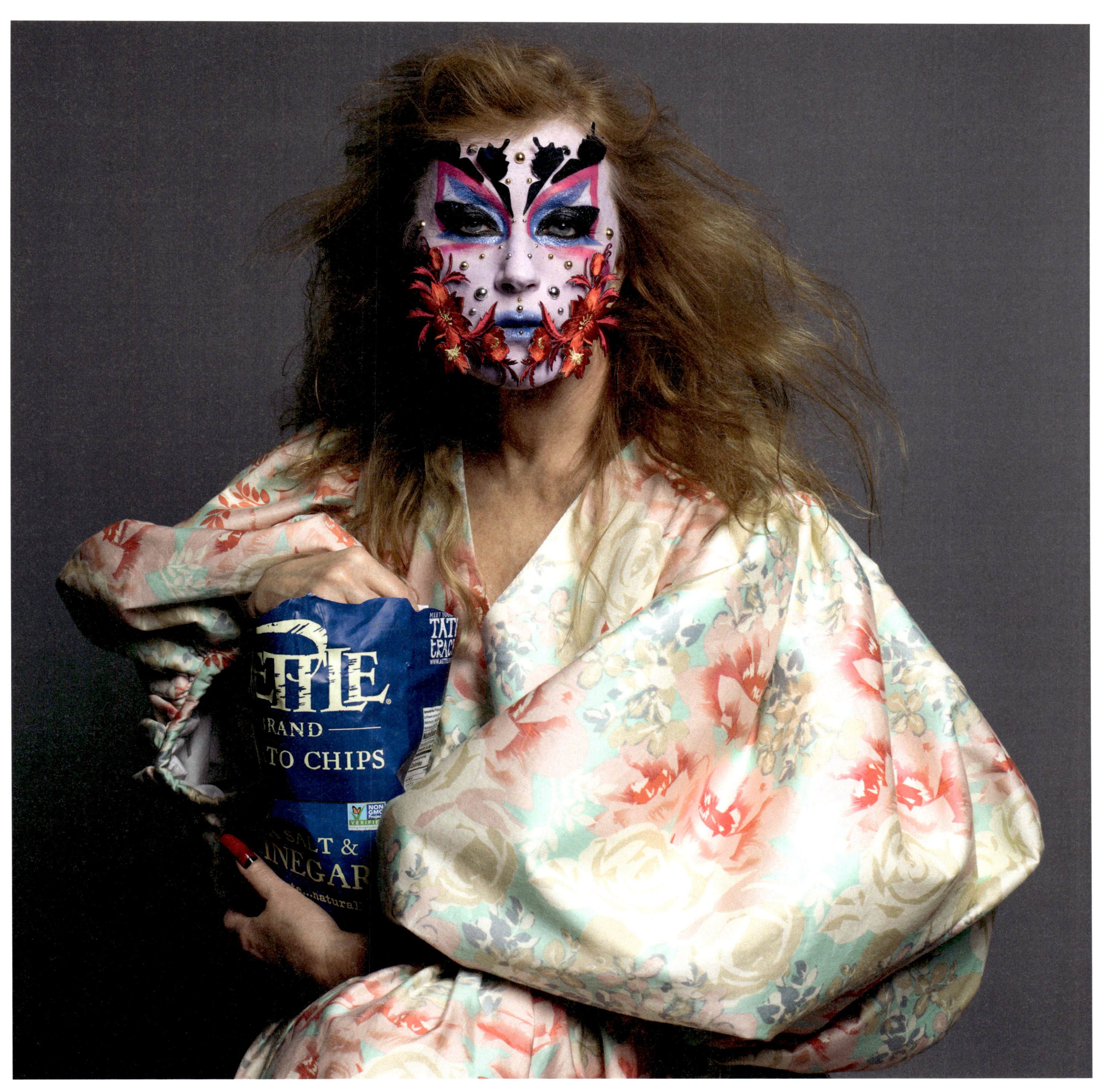
ETTLE
BRAND
TO CHIPS
SALT &
INEGAR

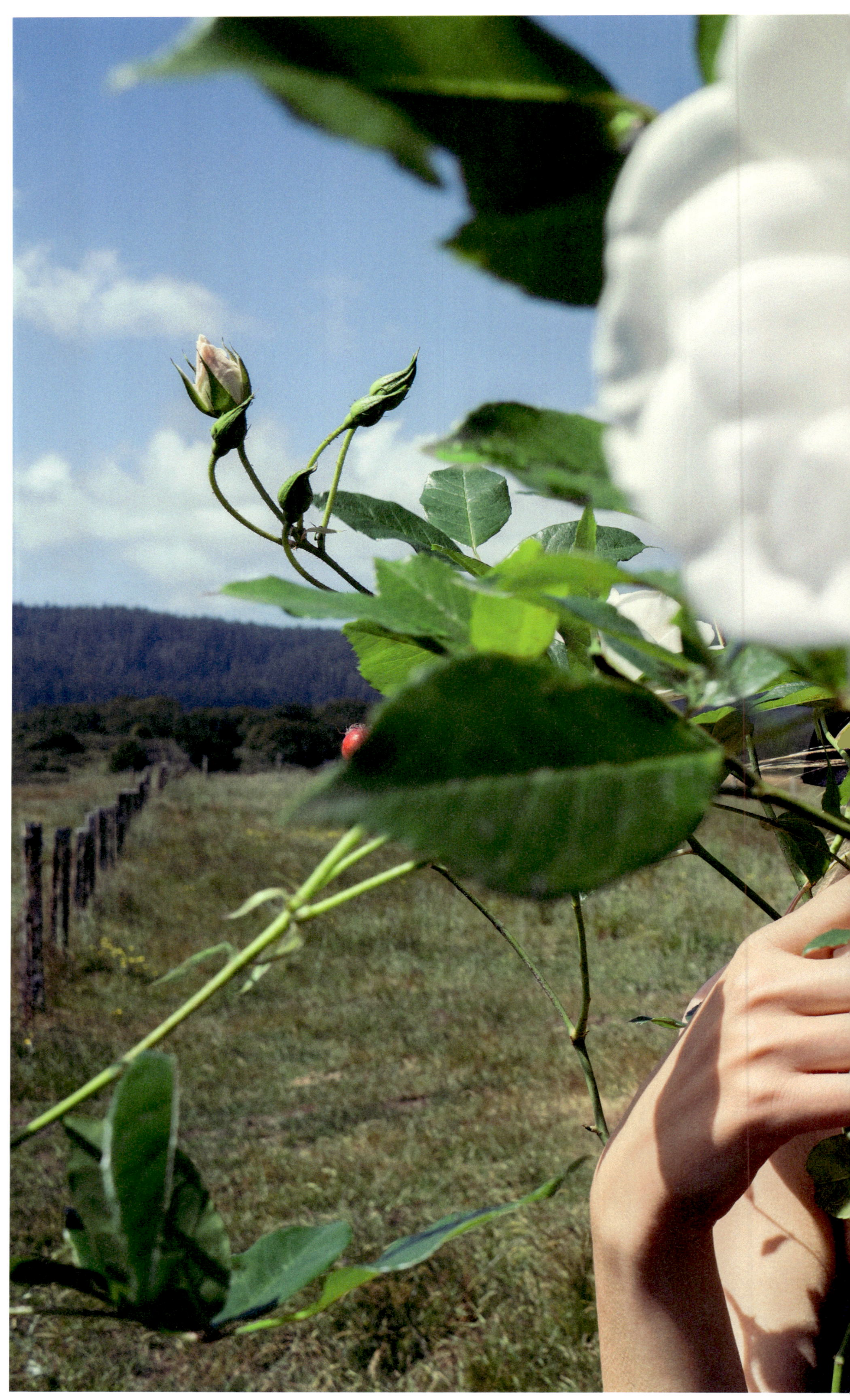

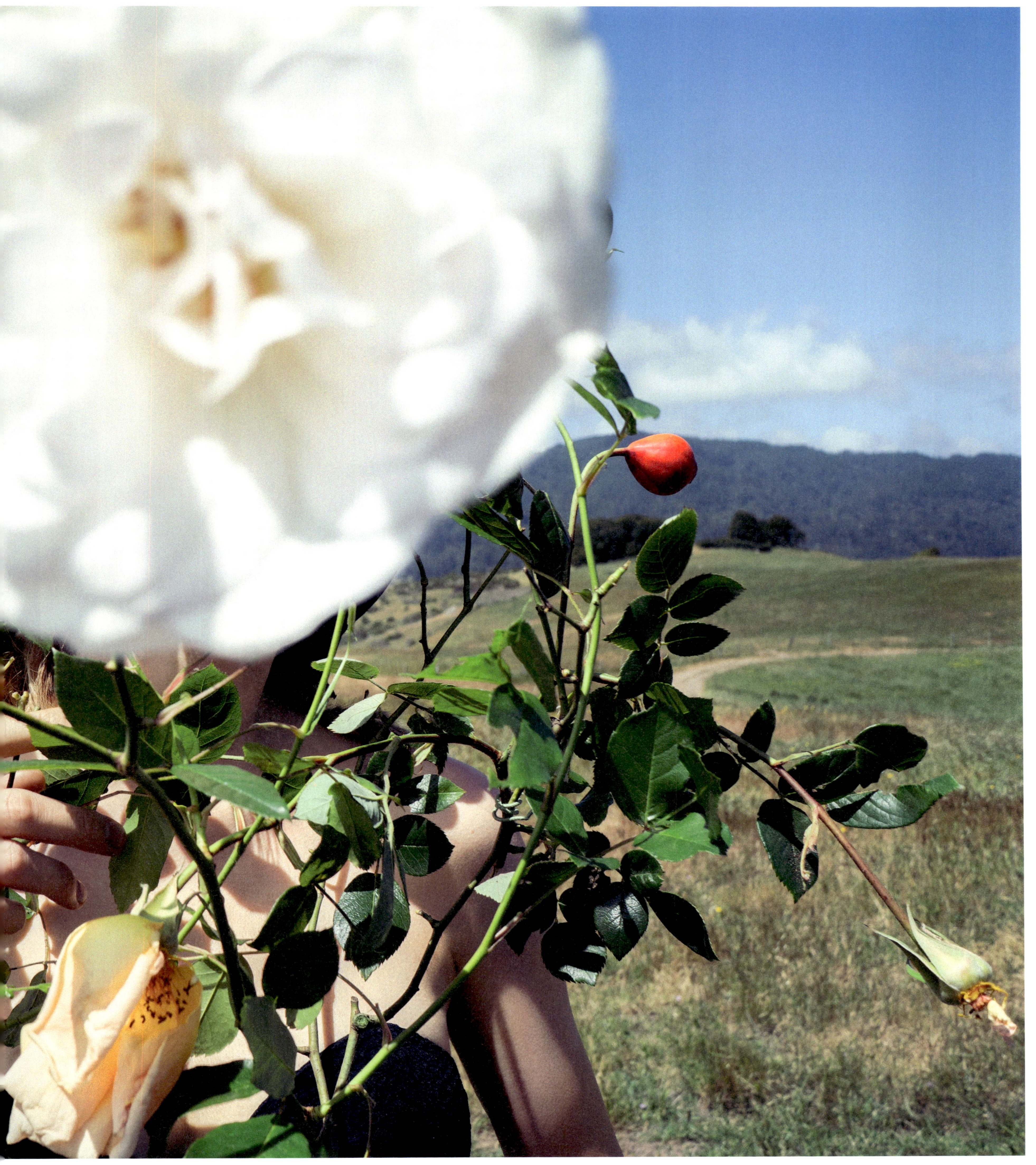

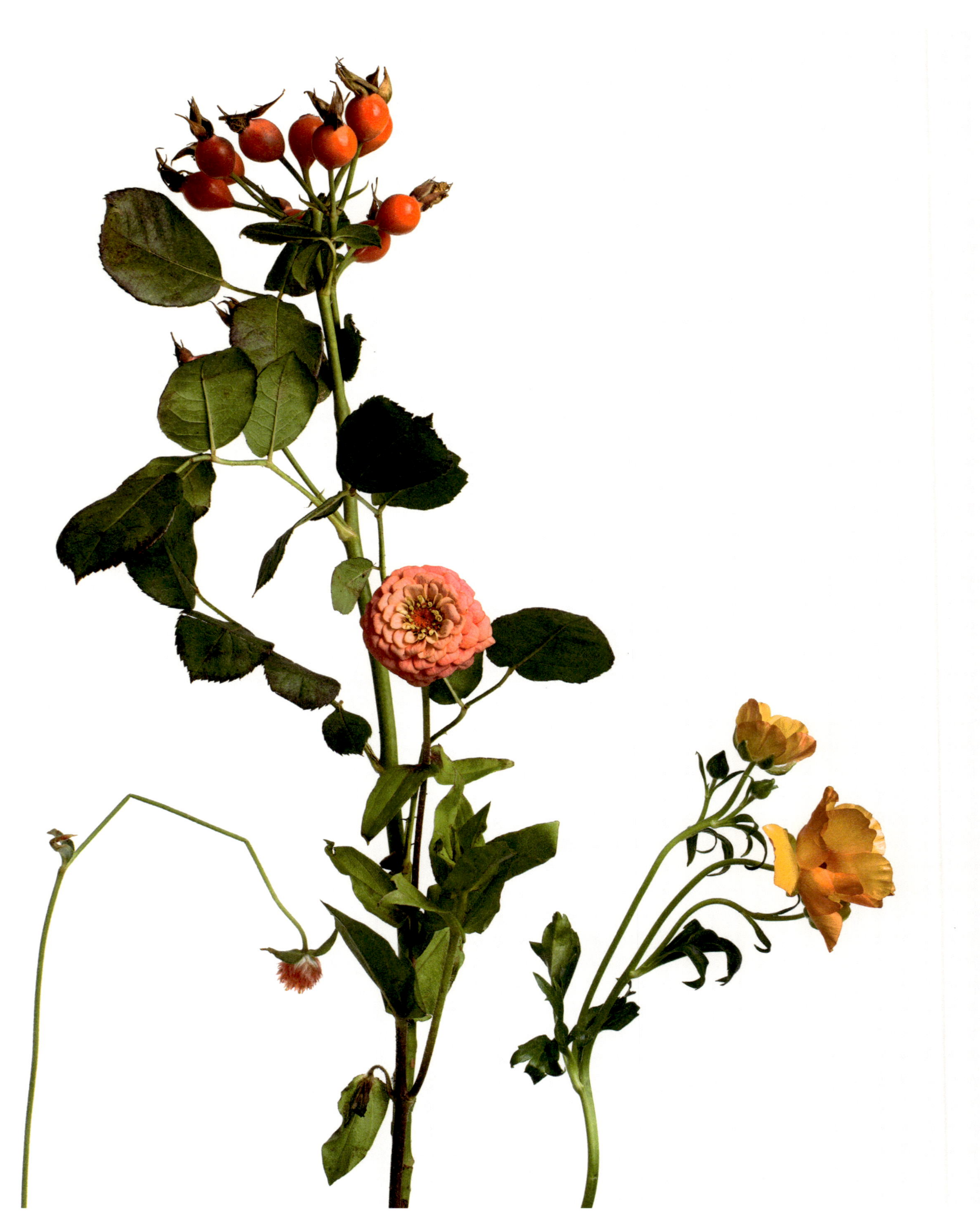

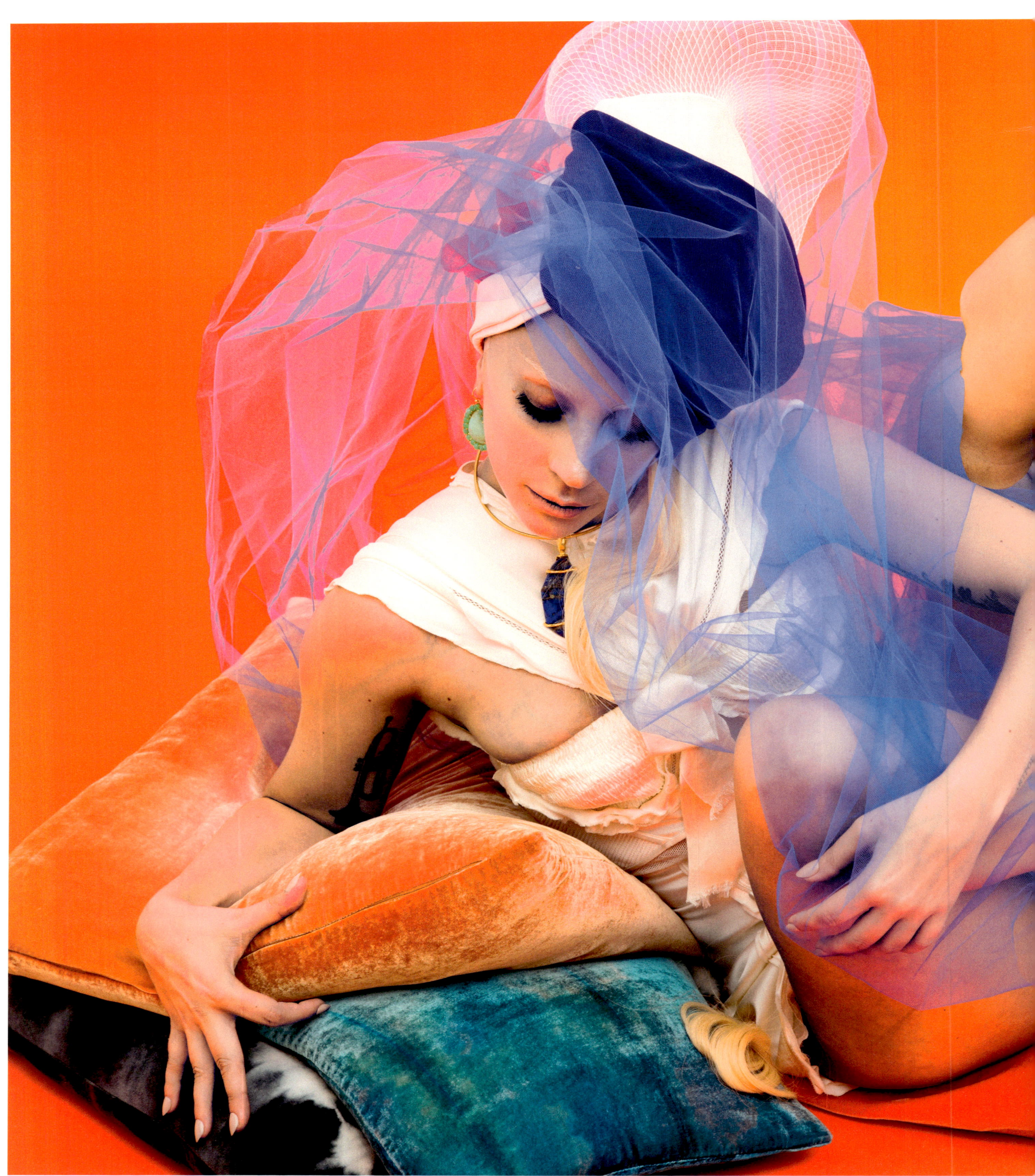

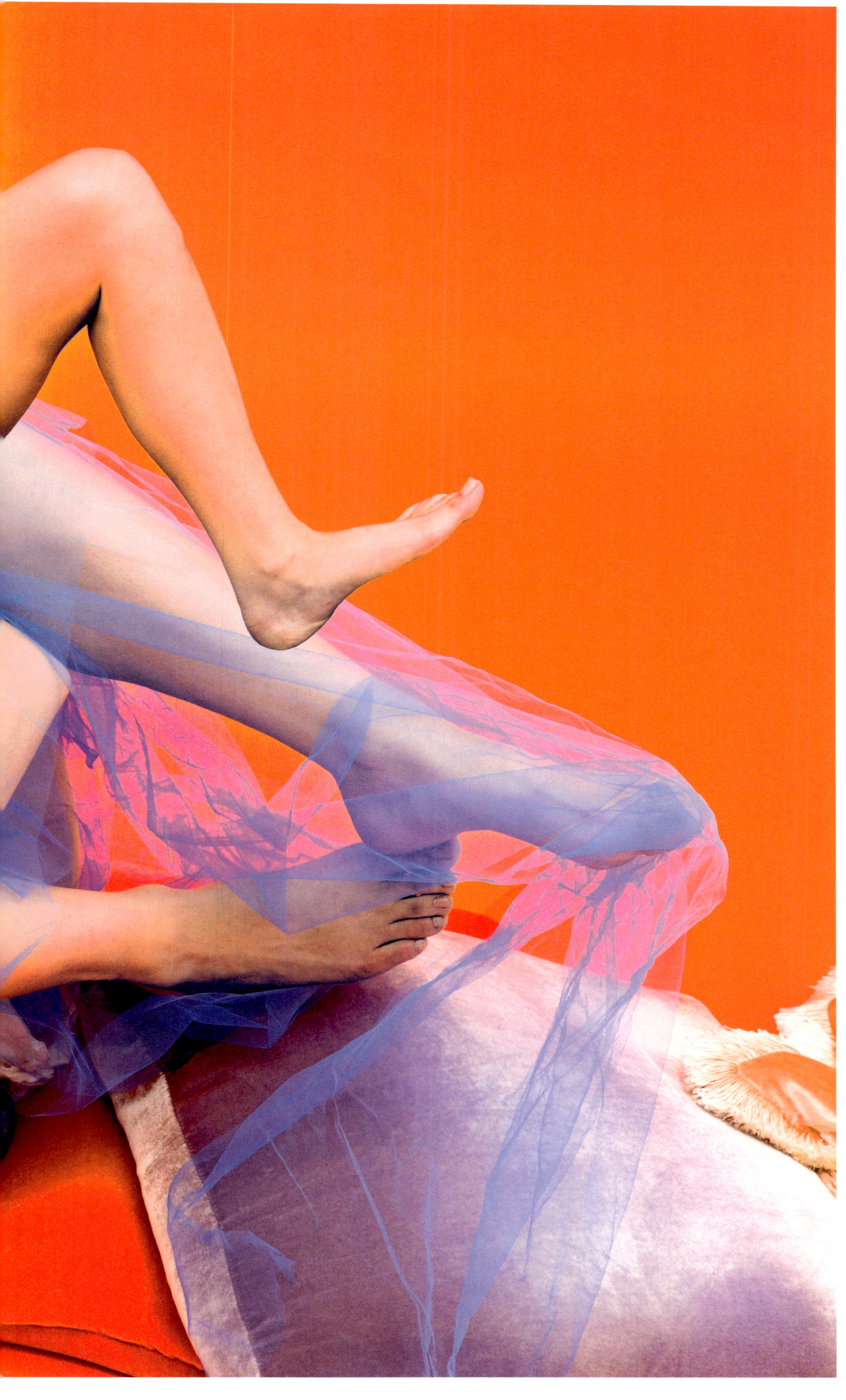

Inez & Vinoodh (b.1963 / b.1961) are one of the most significant figures in contemporary fashion photography, widely known for the introduction of digital manipulation into the fashion industry in the early 1990s. At a time when such technologies had primarily been used in advertising, and the dominant aesthetic was entwined with the 'grunge' movement, Inez & Vinoodh re-imagined these tools for their own use, pioneering a new colourful and fantastical canon to the applause of both the fashion and art industry. Whilst today it is harder to acknowledge the weight of such a shift in a culture driven by seamless technology, it is rare to find a corner of a name or brand in popular culture that has not been touched by the work of Inez & Vinoodh in some way.

Inez & Vinoodh have created ad campaigns for an innumerable list of leading brands that include Christian Dior, Yves Saint Laurent, Gucci, Louis Vuitton, and Chanel, and have photographed personalities such as Kate Moss, Lady Gaga, Tom Cruise, Rihanna, Kanye West, and Paul McCartney. Their work has also been exhibited in galleries and museums internationally including the Stedelijk Museum and Van Gogh Museum in Amsterdam, the Hayward Gallery in London, the Deichtorhallen in Hamburg, and the Whitney Museum of Contemporary Art in New York. A retrospective show titled *Pretty Much Everything 1985–2010* began its international tour at FOAM, Amsterdam in the summer of 2010 and has since travelled to the Pavilion Bienal in Sao Paulo, the Dallas Contemporary in Dallas, and Fotografiska in Stockholm.

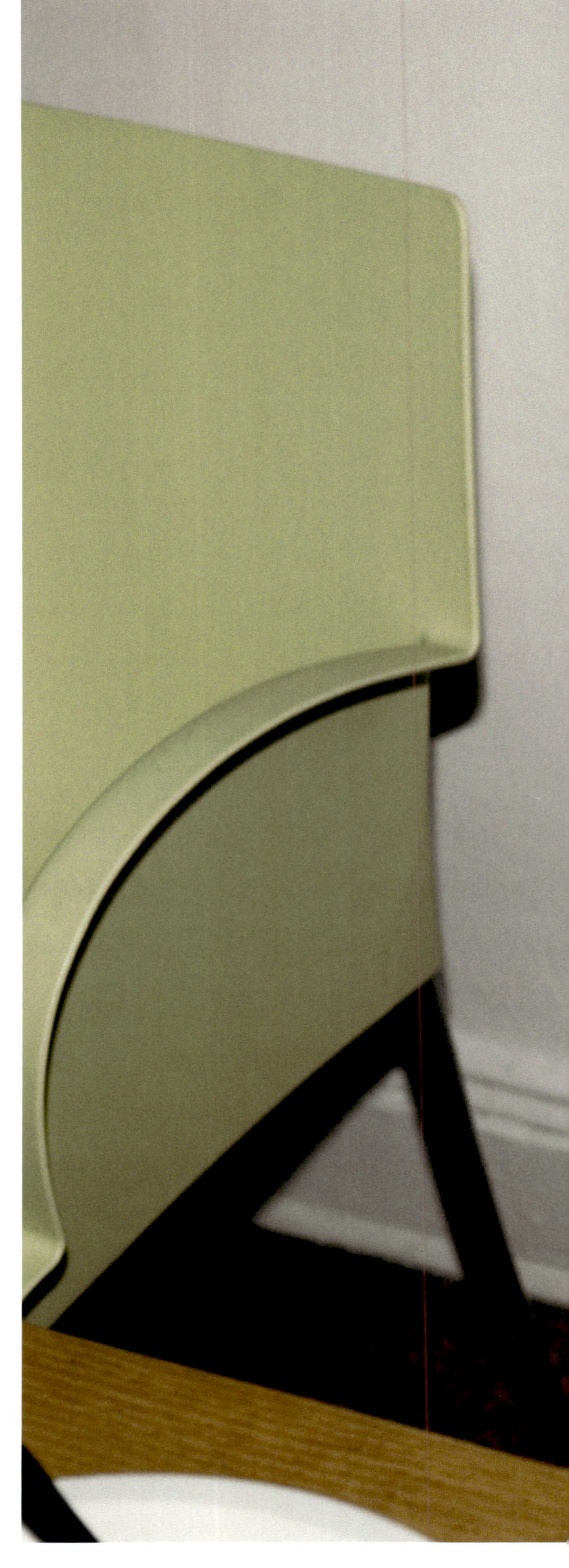

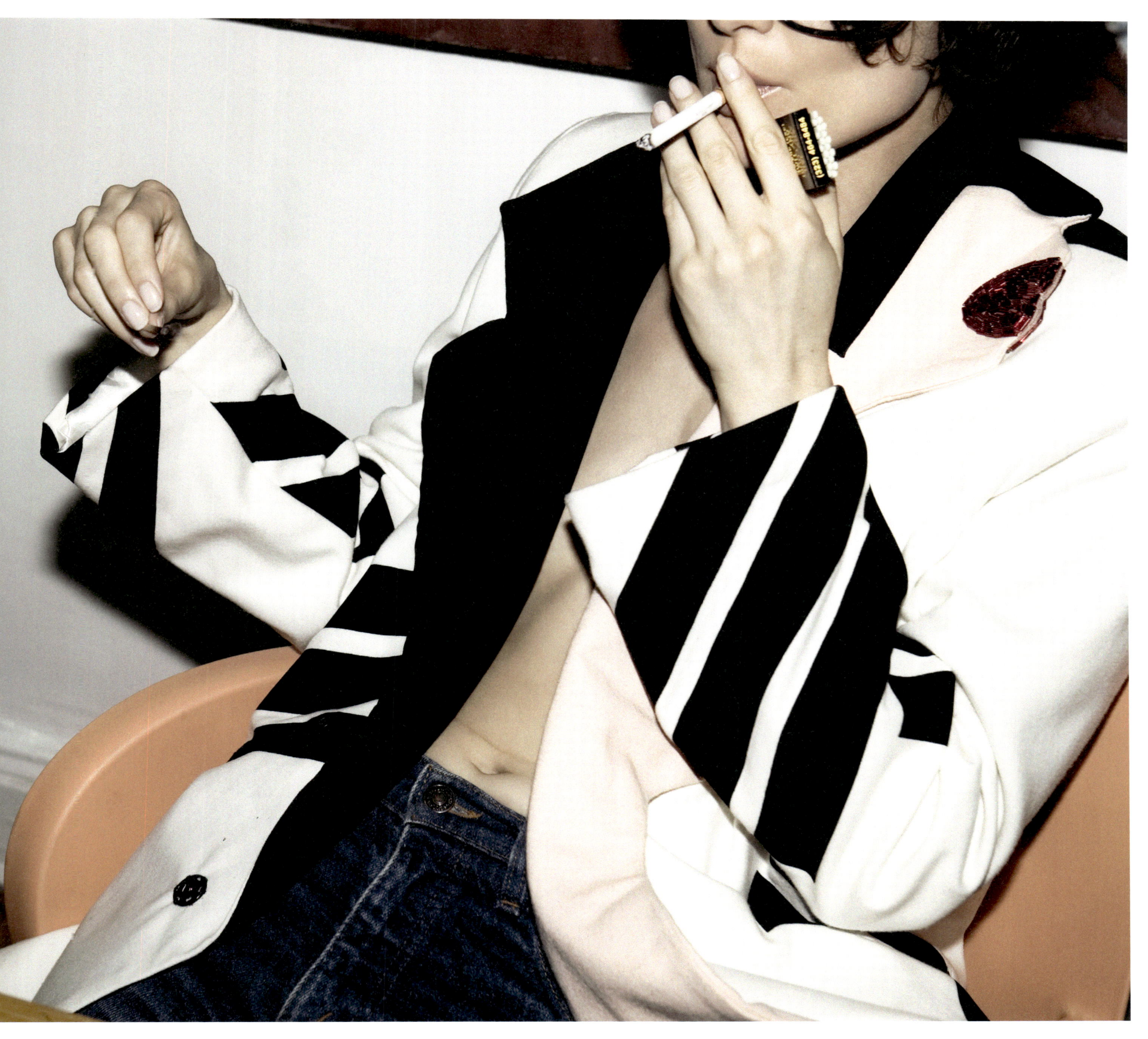

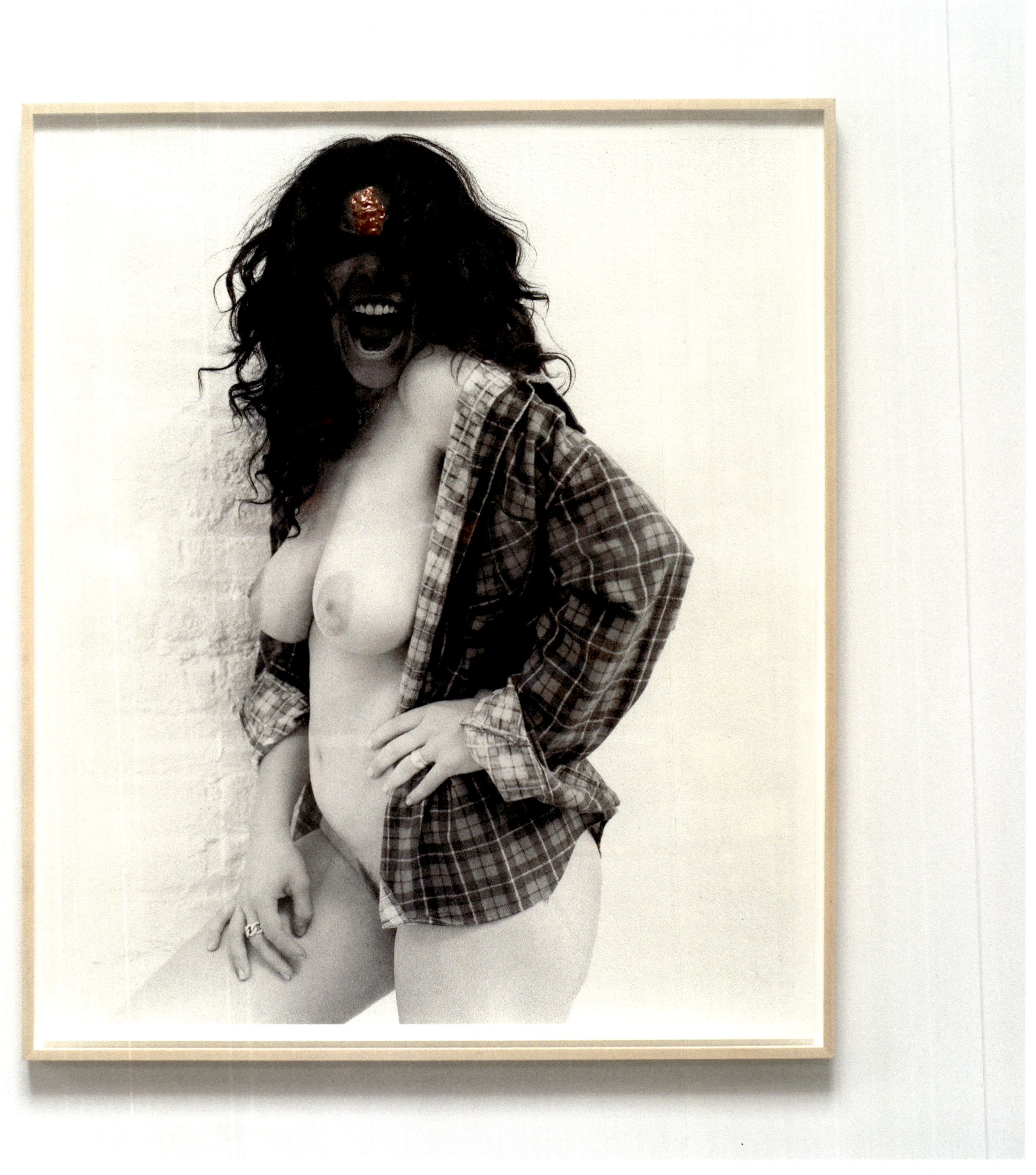

EXPLODE (in collaboration with Eugene van Lamsweerde), 2005